Henry Ford

The Man Who Put the World on Wheels

By Linda Armstrong

Published in the United States of America
by the Hameray Publishing Group, Inc.

Text © Linda Armstrong
Maps © Hameray Publishing Group, Inc.
Published 2009

Publisher: Raymond Yuen
Series Editors: Adria F. Klein and Alan Trussell-Cullen
Project Editor: Kaitlyn Nichols
Designers: Lois Stanfield and Linda Lockowitz
Map Designer: Barry Age

Photo Credits: AP: pages 16, 18-19
Corbis: front cover and pages 4, 8, 12
Getty: back cover and pages 20, 23, 26-27, 31, 33

All rights reserved. No part of this publication may be reproduced
or transmitted in any form or by any means without permission in
writing from the publisher. Reproduction of any part of this book,
through photocopy, recording, or any other mechanical
retrieval system without the written permission of the publisher,
is an infringement of the copyright law.

ISBN 978-1-60559-062-2

Printed in China

1 2 3 4 5 SIP 13 12 11 10 09

Contents

Chapter 1	**On the Road to Detroit**	5
Chapter 2	**Born to Be a Mechanic**	7
Chapter 3	**Keeping the Dream Alive**	11
Chapter 4	**Knocking Out Bricks**	14
Chapter 5	**A Car for Everyone**	17
Chapter 6	**Miracle at Highland Park**	22
Chapter 7	**The Bumpy Road to Success**	25
Chapter 8	**Darkness at Fair Lane**	30
Timeline		34
Glossary		36
Learn More		38
Index		39

▲ A steam engine used on farms in the late 1800's.

Chapter 1

On the Road to Detroit

Their farm wagon creaked as the horses pulled it along the rutted road. The boy sitting up front knew the road to Detroit well. He and his father made the eight mile drive often. Sometimes, the whole family came. This time, the boy and his father were alone. The boy was quiet. He was most likely thinking about his mother. She had died a few months before, and he missed her very much.

Suddenly, he heard something strange. A steam farm engine was chugging down the road! Before his father could stop him, the boy jumped down and ran beside the steam engine shouting questions up to the driver. He had to know how the steam engine worked.

The boy was Henry Ford. That July day in 1876, he was thirteen years old.

Many years later, Ford would help to change the world. Because of his ideas, horse drawn wagons would disappear. People would ride in cars. Highways would replace dirt roads. There would be gas stations, parking lots, and **suburbs**.

Of course, young Henry could not know that. He just knew that he was very excited to see a machine that could do the work of horses!

Chapter 2

Born to Be a Mechanic

Henry Ford was born on July 30, 1863. He was the oldest of six children. His family lived on a farm near Dearborn, Michigan.

7

▲ Henry Ford's birthplace is now a museum open to the public.

Henry's father loved the land, and he wanted his children to love it, too. But even as a boy, the thing that Henry wanted to do most of all was to see how things worked.

This often got him into trouble. One time he and his friends built a waterwheel. They then built a dam in a creek near his house so the water in the creek would turn the waterwheel. The waterwheel helped Henry learn more about machines, but the dam made the creek flood the land around it. Another time Henry and some other boys tried to build a steam boiler but it blew up and left Henry with a scar on his cheek.

> *A steam boiler uses heat to turn water into steam. Many machines like the farm machine Henry had seen as a young boy used steam made by a steam boiler to make them work.*

Henry's mother said he was born to be a **mechanic**. His father didn't agree. He hoped Henry would run the farm, but Henry was more interested in building machines than planting and plowing. When he was sixteen, Henry left home and hiked down the road to Detroit. He was heading for the city where he could learn to be a mechanic.

> "Anyone who stops learning is old, whether at twenty or eighty. Anyone who keeps learning stays young. The greatest thing in life is to keep your mind young."
> —Henry Ford

Chapter 3

Keeping the Dream Alive

Henry Ford became an **apprentice** in a machine shop in Detroit. When Ford finished his training, he moved back home. He had grown from a curious boy into a skilled young man. He worked for a steam engine company and helped the neighbors with repairs to their farm machines.

At a dance, Henry Ford met a special girl, Clara Jane Bryant. From the moment he saw Clara, he knew he loved her. They were married on April 11, 1888. The newlyweds lived on some land that Henry's father had given him.

The couple was happy. But Henry Ford

▲ Henry Ford at twenty-five, a young man with big dreams.

couldn't forget his dream of building a machine that could roll down the road all by itself without any horses to pull it.

One day, on a trip to the city, Ford saw one of the first **internal combustion engines**. It was smaller, lighter, and quieter than a steam engine. It was exactly what Ford had been looking for, and he wanted to learn more about it.

> *The internal combustion engine burns, or combusts, fuel* inside *the engine. The burning fuel turns into gasses. As these gasses expand, they push on pistons and make the engine go. It is different than a steam engine. In a steam engine, combustion happens in a fire box* outside *the engine. Burning fuel heats water to create steam, which drives the engine. Steam engines are larger, heavier, and noisier than internal combustion engines.*

Chapter 4

Knocking Out Bricks

Clara Ford told her husband that he should follow his dream. So in 1891, they moved to Detroit. Ford took a job at a **power house** and worked on internal combustion engines in his spare time.

Soon, their son, Edsel, was born and Ford needed more money. He started teaching classes for young mechanics at night. Through one of his students, he met a man who was working on a new kind of "horseless carriage." Ford was so excited that he rented a small brick building and started to build an automobile of his own. He called it a **Quadricycle** because it had four bicycle wheels. His friends often came by to help. Sometimes, they worked all night.

Finally, the car was finished and they were ready to try it out. It was near dawn and the streets were quiet. Ford and a friend tried to push the Quadricycle out of the building, but it wouldn't fit through the door. So Ford grabbed an ax and began knocking out the bricks to make the door wider!

> *"Obstacles are those frightful things you see when you take your eyes off your goal."*
> —Henry Ford

As Clara watched, the little engine sputtered to life and the Quadricycle putted down the street.

In the weeks that followed, many people in Detroit saw Ford driving his Quadricycle and wanted to find out more about it. Ford began to think he could build cars for a living, so he quit his job at the power house. Unfortunately success wouldn't come as easily as he hoped.

▲ **Henry Ford driving his Quadricycle.**

Chapter 5

A Car for Everyone

Five years later, Ford's idea of making cars was not looking so good. He was out of work and almost out of money. But he was not ready to give up. He knew automobile races were great **advertising** for cars, so Ford entered a big race at the Grosse Pointe Track.

Most people thought Ford was crazy. He had never raced before. The other driver, Alexander Winton, had already won many races. When the cars took off, eight thousand people cheered. Winton shot ahead. Suddenly, there was a puff of smoke. Winton's car slowed and Ford zoomed by to win the race!

Ford's courage paid off. Tom Cooper, a champion bicyclist who had become interested in automobile racing, said he wanted to work with Ford. Together, they built two fast cars. They hired a young man named Barney Oldfield to drive for them. Oldfield set a speed record in Ford's 999.

Success on the track helped Ford raise money to start the Ford Motor Company. His company made good automobiles and they sold well. Many other companies also made good cars. To stand out, Ford needed a special product.

Henry Ford stands beside his 999 racer; Barney Oldfield is in the car.

19

At that time most cars were just for the rich. Ford's dream was to make a car that everyone could afford. In 1908 the company introduced the Model T. It changed everything. Model Ts were sturdy and simple cars. But best of all, everybody could afford them.

▲ Henry Ford proudly stands with a newly made Model T.

By 1920 half of the cars in the country were Model Ts. Over the years, Ford sold more than fifteen million of them.

The Model T first went on sale in 1908. Ford named his automobiles using the letters of the alphabet, starting with the Model A. But a number of models were just prototypes that were never developed for sale. That is why, although T is the twentieth letter of the alphabet, the Model T was only the ninth model to go into production. People also called the Model T the "Tin Lizzie" and the "Flivver." When Ford was ready to begin a new model to follow the Model T, he didn't go to the next letter of the alphabet. His new model was a very different kind of automobile so he decided to start at the beginning of the alphabet again and call it the Model A.

Chapter 6

Miracle at Highland Park

Now everybody wanted a Model T. Ford had to find a faster way to put them together.

One of his men told him about an **assembly line** he had seen at a meatpacking company. Ford agreed that the idea might work for cars. Leaders in his plant started breaking hard jobs down into simpler ones. Workers at the plant made suggestions, too.

> "Nothing is particulary hard if you divide it into small jobs."
> —Henry Ford

▲ Workers putting together parts of a Model T on an assembly line.

By 1913 the assembly line at Ford's Highland Park Plant was complete. Parts and cars moved from one station to the next. Each worker did one small task. For example, one person would drill a hole. The next person would place a bolt into the hole, and a third person would put a nut on it and tighten it. Moving belts carried parts down the line.

The new assembly line worked very well, but it was not perfect. The jobs were simple, but they were boring. Workers often stayed home. Many quit after a few months. Missing workers slowed the line down.

In 1914 Ford thought of a way to keep good workers. He offered to pay better **wages** than other auto companies and he shortened the work day. He even offered to share company **profits** with workers.

Other business leaders thought Ford was crazy, but his bold move worked. His workers showed up, and they stayed on the job. The assembly line sped up production and more cars rolled out of Ford's plant every year.

Chapter 7

The Bumpy Road to Success

Henry Ford was famous now. Newspapers and magazines printed dozens of articles about him. People loved the fact that although he was rich and successful, he still loved country dancing and home cooking. The articles pointed out that Ford succeeded because he stubbornly refused to give up. But in time that stubbornness became a problem.

In the 1920s, other car makers started selling models that were more comfortable and easier to drive than Ford's cars. Ford's son Edsel now worked for his father. He tried to get his father to drop the Model T.

He even worked with a designer to build a beautiful new car. Edsel thought his father would be pleased, but he was wrong. Ford kicked the car and had it taken away. The Model T had put ordinary people on wheels, and Ford was not ready to give it up.

But by 1927, Ford could see that his son was right. Ford was losing sales to other companies. It was time to say goodbye to the Model T. He worked with Edsel to design his next car, the Model A. It did not change the world, but it sold well.

◀ Henry and Edsel Ford at a car show in 1928.

During the 1930s **labor unions** became very powerful. All of the other car companies signed **contracts** with them. Henry Ford didn't believe in unions, so he wouldn't sign.

> ### Labor Unions
> *A labor union, also called a trade union, is a group of workers who have joined together to make employers offer better pay and working conditions.*

On May 26, 1937, union leaders carrying signs posed for a newspaper picture near Ford's plant. Ford security men went to stop the photo from being taken and they beat up the union leaders. This happened on a bridge from the parking lot to the plant. It became known as "The Battle of the **Overpass**."

Four years later, workers held a **sit-down strike** in Ford's plant. They refused to work until their demands were met. Ford could see that he had no choice, so he gave in and signed the contracts.

> *"Coming together is a beginning; keeping together is progress; working together is success."*
> —Henry Ford

Chapter 8

Darkness at Fair Lane

Henry Ford was president of the Ford Motor Company into his eighties. In September 1945 his grandson, Henry Ford II, took over as president.

April 7, 1947 was stormy. That night the power went out at **Fair Lane**, the Ford's home. The house's fifty-six rooms were dark. On that stormy night, Henry Ford had a stroke and died in his wife's arms. He was eighty-three. His body was taken to Greenfield Village, a living history museum that Henry Ford had built. About one hundred thousand people came to say goodbye.

Henry Ford in 1940. ▶

Henry Ford made a huge difference in the world. His special gift was his ability to know a great idea when he saw one. He didn't invent the car but he saw what a great thing it would be if everyone could have one. He didn't invent the assembly line but he saw how to make it work in new ways.

Ford wanted to make a machine that moved people. He did that. He also helped to move the world into the Twentieth Century.

> *"Life is a series of experiences, each one of which makes us bigger, even though sometimes it is hard to realize this. For the world was built to develop character, and we must learn that the setbacks and grieves which we endure help us in our marching onward."* —Henry Ford

Timeline

1863   Henry Ford is born, July 30

1879   Leaves home to become a mechanic

1888   Marries Clara Bryant, April 11

1891   Takes a job at a power house in Detroit

1893   Son, Edsel, is born

1896   Tries out the Quadricycle, his first car

1901   Wins race at Grosse Pointe, October 10

1902   Barney Oldfield sets a new speed record in Ford's 999 racer, October 25

1903   Forms the Ford Motor Company

1908   Introduces the Model T (the 9th Ford model), October 1

1913 Runs a moving assembly line for the first time

1914 Henry Ford keeps good workers on his assembly lines by paying better wages and shortening the work day

1920 Half of the cars in the U.S. are Ford Model Ts

1927 Replaces the Model T with the Model A

1937 Ford security men beat up union leaders at the Battle of the Overpass, May 26

1945 Henry Ford's grandson, Henry Ford II, takes over as president of Ford Motor Co.

1947 Henry Ford dies of a stroke at age 83, April 7

Glossary

advertising — telling people about a new product or service

apprentice — a helper who learns by working with an experienced person

assembly line — a way to put products together. Each worker does a single task

contracts — agreements

Fair Lane — Henry Ford's home

internal combustion engines — motors that do not need an outside boiler or electrical power source

labor union — a group that fights for the rights of workers

mechanic	person who fixes machines
overpass	a walking bridge over a road, river, or parking lot
power house	sends out electricity to people in a town
profits	money a company earns
Quadricycle	Henry Ford's first car
sit-down strike	a protest where employees refuse to work until their demands are met
suburbs	housing areas around a big city
wages	money paid to workers

Learn More

Books
Eat My Dust! Henry Ford's First Race
 by Monica Kulling (Random House Books for Young Readers, 2004)
Henry Ford by Wil Mara (Tandem Library, 2004)
Henry Ford by Jeffrey Zuehlke (Lerner Publications, 2007)
Henry Ford: Young Man with Ideas
 by Hazel B. Aird (Aladdin, 1986)

Websites
www.hfmgv.org/EXHIBITS/HF/
www.inventors.about.com/od/fstartinventors/a/HenryFord.htm
www.spartacus.schoolnet.co.uk/USAford.htm

Movies
Henry Ford: Tin Lizzy Tycoon
 (A&E Home Video, 2006)

Visit
Greenfield Village in Dearborn, Michigan

Index

999 18

advertising 17, 36
apprentice 11, 36
assembly line 22, 23, 24, 32, 36
automobile 14, 17, 18, 19

Battle of the Overpass 29

contract 28, 29, 36
Cooper, Tom 18

Dearborn 7
Detroit 5, 10, 11, 14, 16

Fair Lane 30, 36
Ford Motor Company 19, 30
Ford, Clara Jane 11, 14, 15
Ford, Edsel 14, 25, 26, 27

Greenfield Village 30
Grosse Point Track 17

Highland Park Plant 23

internal combustion engine 13, 14, 36

labor unions 28, 36

machine shop 11
mechanic 10, 14, 37
Michigan 7
Model A 27
Model T 20, 21, 22, 25, 26, 27

Oldfield, Barney 18

power house 14, 16, 37
profits 24, 37

Quadricycle 14, 15, 16, 37

races 17

39

sit-down strike 29, 37
speed record 18
steam boiler 9
steam engine 6, 11, 13
stroke 30

waterwheel 9
Winton, Alexander 17